CLEAN BREAK

presents

MERCY FINE

A new play by Shelley Silas

IN SPRING 2004, I spent twelve weeks driving up the motorway at seven every Friday morning, to a beautiful part of Kent. To a city girl like me, whose eyes open wide at the merest glimpse of countryside, it was a day out. I was teaching creative writing to a group of nine women, sometimes fewer, depending on their circumstances i.e. whether they were on leave, working, at University or in the right frame of mind to attend my class. I was doing all of this at HMP East Sutton Park, an open prison. Prior to starting, I had never stepped foot in a prison and had not given much thought to what it was like. From that day on, I thought about it a great deal.

On my first morning, the car broke down. I arrived an hour late. Not good. Especially as one of the prime pieces of advice I was given during training was not to let prisoners down because that happens to them all the time. But they were there, waiting for me in the library, which also doubled up as the dining room. We had tea, and did some good work. When I left, I was told someone would drive me to the station. I assumed it would be one of the staff. I was in fact driven by one of the prisoners. She was a prison driver.

At the time of writing the second draft of this play, HMP East Sutton Park was under threat of closure. It is one of only two open prisons for women in England. It allows offenders a kind of temporary taste of the outside world, before being sent back into a society that often shuns them, often doesn't trust them. Maybe it never trusted them in the first place. Maybe that's part of why they are who they are. The expectation is that many of these women will re-offend. I am a firm believer in going to the source of the problem and dealing with that, not just locking people up and punishing them as if that were a solution. As we know to our cost, locking people away is rarely the answer.

During my weekly sessions, I came to know some extraordinary – and very scared – women, a couple on the verge of release, others with three or four years left of a twelve or fourteen year sentence. I didn't realise how easy it would be for any one of us to end up with a prison sentence, whether for a month or a year, whether for non-payment of fines, shoplifting or drug trafficking. I also knew that unless I committed a crime I would never know what it was like to be a prisoner. And that every prisoner has a different experience, from the woman who said it wasn't the worst thing in the world, to the woman who said it was like boarding school. Some would have preferred to be in a closed prison like Holloway, where they knew where they stood, rather than an open prison like HMP East Sutton Park. So, when it came to writing a play, faced with all the possible routes I could take, I started with my own questions, and one of the biggest fears I came across while doing my research – that of offenders preparing to return into society. *Mercy Fine* is the result.

DEDICATED TO the creative writing group at HMP East Sutton Park, May – July 2004. Thank you for saying yes, for doing the work and making my tea with such enthusiasm. I hope wherever you all are, you are happy and well. And still writing…

THANKS TO everyone at Clean Break. Gillian Sharp, Nigel Fry and George Carruthers at HMP East Sutton Park. Fay Barratt, Lin Coghlan and the creative writing class at Clean Break. Emma Bravo for books. Rebecca Prichard, Jennifer Farmer, Jeanie O'Hare, Claire Grove, Deborah Paige, Stephanie Street, Tanika Gupta, Stella Duffy, Lee Simpson, Martyn Waites, Katie Haines, Natalia Fernandez, Fay Davies, Hansi Smythe, Oberon. Bernie, Cat, Adrienne, Jo, Jess, Zoe, Kim and Crin. Annabelle Apsion, Nathalie Armin, Jenny Jules and Lindy Whiteford, and my friends who listened ad infinitum to my prison tales, and are still listening. Louise, Lynne, Hazel, Bindya. Natasha Betteridge and Donatella Beterati for kebobs and glitter. And Simon, who against all odds got me to the prison on time. Well, almost.

Shelley Silas
September 2005

MERCY FINE

Writer Shelley Silas
Director Natasha Betteridge
Designer Bernadette Roberts
Lighting Designer Catriona Silver
Sound Designer Adrienne Quartly

CAST

Mercy Hazel Holder
Viv Louise Bangay
Frehia/Officer Davis Bindya Solanki
Jean Lynne Verrall

AUTUMN TOUR 2005

Wednesday 5 to Saturday 8 October
Birmingham Repertory Theatre, The Door
Box Office 0121 236 4455
Sign language interpreted performance 6 October
Post show discussion 7 October
www.birmingham-rep.co.uk

Monday 10 to Wednesday 12 October
York Theatre Royal Studio
Box Office 01904 623568
Post show discussion 11 October
Sign language interpreted performance 12 October
www.yorktheatreroyal.co.uk

Thursday 20 to Saturday 22 October
Salisbury Playhouse, Salberg Studio
Box Office 01722 320333
Sign language interpreted performance and post show discussion 20 October
www.salisburyplayhouse.com

Tuesday 8 to Saturday 26 November
Southwark Playhouse
Box Office 08700 601761
Post show discussion 17 November
Sign language interpreted performance 23 November
www.southwarkplayhouse.co.uk

Performances at women's prisons and education work will also take place during the tour.

CLEAN BREAK WOULD like to thank the following for their support with *Mercy Fine*: the staff and women at HMP East Sutton Park, Rebecca Prichard, Jeanie O'Hare, Tara Hull, Annabelle Apsion, Nathalie Armin, Jenny Jules, Lindy Whiteford, Lisa Makin, Bridget Irving, David Maloney from Chanel, Restore Furniture Aid Tottenham Hale, Dr Ken Godbert from Hereford PCT, Virgin Airlines, Jas Denny and Peter Berry from HSAG, and the Stage Department, Royal Court Theatre. Trees provided by Simon Levey from Richmond Park.

CLEAN BREAK

Clean Break is a theatre, education and new writing company. We use theatre for personal and political change, working with women whose lives have been affected by the criminal justice system. We believe passionately that engaging in theatre can create new opportunities for these women and develop their personal, social, artistic and professional skills.

Clean Break was founded by two women in prison in 1979. From its roots as a small-scale fringe theatre company, it has grown today to become a critically-acclaimed new writing theatre company producing original work based on a unique research and development process. The production and new writing programme is now complemented by a highly respected and innovative year-round education and training programme. We work with women offenders and women at risk of offending due to drug or alcohol use or mental health needs. The education work takes place in women's prisons and with community groups, and we have a year-round programme of courses at our purpose-built studios in North London.

Clean Break runs an innovative programme of theatre performances and new writing projects, drama-based education and specialist support, professional development and training, and advocacy.

For more information about Clean Break visit our website at
www.cleanbreak.org.uk

You can keep in touch by joining the mailing list through our website or by contacting us on **020 7482 8600**.

CLEAN BREAK is supported by Arts Council England, Camden Council, Association of London Government and is a member of ITC.

MAKE A DONATION and help us make a difference to more women's lives

Clean Break aims to bring about change directly in the lives of the women we work with and, at a national level, through changing attitudes to women and crime through theatre, education and new writing. Our services are much in demand and we have ambitious plans for:

- more education work, affecting the lives of individual women and supporting them through their education at Clean Break
- new writing projects for professional and non-professional women writers
- increased work with young women offenders and those at risk of offending
- increased touring to theatres and prisons with accompanying education work
- increased links with women's prisons across the country
- training for artists and criminal justice professionals wanting to learn more about our ways of working.

We invite you to contact us to discuss supporting one or more of these areas with a one-off or regular donation. We rely heavily on the generous support of our funders and donors. By making a financial contribution to Clean Break, you can make a difference to the lives of the women and their families. If you would like to discuss Clean Break's programme further and how you could get involved contact Lucy Perman MBE, Executive Director, on 020 7482 8600.

Alternatively you can donate direct on-line via our website at www.cleanbreak.org.uk or through a secure e-fundraising service provided by the Charities Aid Foundation at www.givenow.org

Board of directors
Paulette Randall (Chair), Joan Scanlon (Vice Chair), Sylvia Amanquah, Jude Boyles, Sarah Daniels, Lorraine Faissal, Rahila Gupta, Sonali Naik, Jeanie O'Hare, Kate O'Rourke, Sharon Shea.

Patrons
Paul Boateng MP, Carmen Callil, Dame Judi Dench, Sir Richard Eyre CBE, Barbara Hosking CBE, Baroness Helena Kennedy QC, Ann Mitchell, Yve Newbold LLB, Baroness Usha Prashar CBE, Baroness Vivien Stern CBE, Janet Suzman, Emma Thompson, Harriet Walter CBE.

Contact
Clean Break	Tel: 020 7482 8600
2 Patshull Road	Fax: 020 7482 8611
London	general@cleanbreak.org.uk
NW5 2LB	www.cleanbreak.org.uk

Registered company number 2690758 / Registered charity number 1017560

FOR MERCY FINE

Mercy Fine is commissioned and produced by Clean Break.

Company Stage Manager **Jo Rawlinson**
Deputy Stage Manager **Jess Gow**
Assistant Stage Manager **Zoe King**
Relights Technician **Crin Claxton**
Stage Management Trainee **Kim Raper**

Casting Adviser **Amy Ball**
Marketing Consultants **Martha Oakes PR**
Press Consultant **Bridget Thornborrow**
Workshop Leader **Fay Barratt**
Movement Consultant **Liz Rankin**
Publicity Designer **Frolic Design**
Sign Interpreted Performances **Jeni Draper**
Promotional Photographer **Amelia Troubridge**
Production Photographer **Sarah Ainslie**
Set Construction and Painters **Capital Scenery Ltd**

FOR CLEAN BREAK

Executive Director **Lucy Perman MBE**
Administrative Producer **Helen Pringle**
Head of Education **Anna Herrmann**
Head of New Writing **Lucy Morrison**
Production Manager **Bendy Ashfield**
Education Manager (Accredited Courses) **Imogen Ashby**
Education Manager (Short Courses and Progression Routes) **Kerri Mesner**
Student Support Manager **Jackie Stewart**
Student Support Worker **Ella Bullingham**
Girls and Young Women's Development Worker **Jo Whitehouse**
Funding Co-ordinator **Emma Goodway**
Literary and Production Assistant **Sarah Nixey**
Executive Assistant **Esther Poyer**
Education Assistant **Tracey Daley**
Finance Administrator **Won Fyfe**
Office Administrator **Sam McNeil**

WHILE ELEMENTS OF *Mercy Fine* are inspired by real life events, all characters, their names and incidents portrayed are entirely fictitious. Any resemblance to the name, character or history of any person is coincidental and unintentional.

BIOGRAPHIES

Louise Bangay Viv

Louise's theatre work includes Cenchreis in Poor Beck by Joanna Laurens (Soho Theatre and The Other Place) and Witch in Macbeth (Albery Theatre and RST), both for the Royal Shakespeare Company in their last season. Other theatre includes Sara in Ben Hur (BAC); Lady Capulet in Romeo and Juliet (Northcott Theatre, Exeter); Cornelia in Mouth to Mouth (Royal Court at the Albery); Ivana in Anyroad (Bridewell); Two (Ross Festival and Brazilian Tour); Still Life (One-Woman Show, London Play Festival); Self Accusation (Sadler's Wells); Naschendo (Tricycle); Horace, Katerina and The Cenci (all the Lyric, Hammersmith); Miss Julie (Young Vic); Rick's Bar Casablanca (Whitehall Theatre); The Vanek Plays (Lyric and Prague). Television work includes The Bill, Imogen's Face, Bliss, Trainer and Models Required.

Natasha Betteridge Director

Natasha trained at RADA and was previously Artistic Producer at Northampton Theatres Trust, Associate Director at West Yorkshire Playhouse and Resident Director at the Orange Tree Theatre Room. Recent productions include Tim Fountain, Sex Addict (Royal Court), and the world premiere of Hotboi by Tim Fountain, starring Bette Bourne (Soho Theatre). She has also directed the world premières of Girl, Watching by Jyll Bradley (Birmingham Rep), Untouchable by Simon Burt (Bush Theatre) and A Listening Heaven by Torben Betts (SJT Scarborough). She has strong links with Chinese theatre and was the first European to direct a new play in China – Li Ting's You Once Passed Me By (at the Sitchuan Peoples' Theatre). She is currently directing a short film for ITV Wales.

Hazel Holder Mercy

Hazel Holder trained at North Herts College, Hitchin and Mountview Theatre School, London and upon graduating from Mountview she joined the cast of Carmen Jones at the Old Vic. She then took the title role in The Belle of the Belfast City at the Orange Tree Theatre, London. Other theatre credits include Maskarade with Talawa, jazz musical Ain't Misbehavin' at the Lyric Shaftesbury Avenue and national tours with Sphinx Theatre Company in the Jean Rhys play Voyage in the Dark and Black Mime Theatre's devised production of Mourning Song. Upon completing the Intensive Course at The School of the Science of Acting Hazel took the role of Iris in the RSC's international tour of The Tempest and also understudied Ariel. Since then she has played the role of The Minstrel in the Young Vic production of The Sleeping Beauty recreating the role on Broadway, New York. Other recent credits include The Trojan Women and The Lion and the Jewel for Collective Artistes and Judge John Deed for BBC TV. Other work includes several guest leads on TV and BBC

Radio 4 Drama and the New Writers Project at the Royal Court Theatre and presenting and producing for BBC Three Counties Radio. Hazel is a member of The Helen Chadwick Group and is also lead vocalist with jazz/swing band Ronnie Scott's Rejects.

Adrienne Quartly Sound Designer

Formerly a radio producer, Adrienne now works as a freelance Creative Sound Designer. She has created soundscapes for many productions including 93.2FM (Royal Court Theatre), Hideaway for Complicité, Woyzeck and Tejas Verdes (the Gate Theatre), Lady Luck for Lucy Porter (Assembly Rooms, Edinburgh Festival Fringe 2004), Attempts On Her Life (BAC), Jarman Garden and National Alien Office (Riverside Studios), Forgotten Voices (Southwark Playhouse), Habeas Corpus and Quartermaine's Terms (Royal Theatre Northampton and Salisbury Playhouse), Circo Ridiculoso's Inflated Ideas (National Circus Bites Tour) and The Last Waltz Season (Arcola Theatre). As a cellist Adrienne is featured on Piano Magic's album Artists Rifles.

Bernadette Roberts Designer

Bernadette has designed extensively for theatre, opera, dance and television. Theatre credits include Two Step (Almeida), Dead Funny (Nottingham Playhouse), Stig of the Dump and 7x7 (West Yorkshire Playhouse). Her production design credits for television include Every Time You Look At Me (BBC), A&E series 2 & 3 (Granada), EastEnders (BBC), Still Here (6 Films for the Windrush season, BBC), The Estate Agents (Channel 4) and costume design for International King of Sports (Channel 4). She has also taught design for the Royal Opera House, both here and abroad.

Shelley Silas Writer

Shelley was born in Calcutta and grew up in North London. Her plays include Calcutta Kosher (Kali Theatre – Southwark Playhouse, UK tour, Theatre Royal Stratford East); Falling, (Bush Theatre – Pearson writer-in-residence 2002), Shrapnel (Steam Industry – BAC). Her plays for Radio Four include The Sound of Silence, Calcutta Kosher, Ink, Collective Fascination and Nothing Happened (with Luke Sorba). She adapted Hanan al-Shaykh's novel Only in London and co-adapted Paul Scott's The Raj Quartet (with John Harvey). She compiled and edited an anthology of short stories, 12 Days, published by Virago. Current projects include a new play for Tamasha Theatre.

Catriona Silver Lighting Designer

Catriona has worked previously with Natasha Betteridge and Clean Break on Inside Out by Tanika Gupta. Other work includes The Lion and the Jewel (Young Vic Young Genius Season), Women of Owu (National Tour for Collective Artistes), Just in Name (Birmingham Rep), The Associate and Achilles

(National Theatre), Neville's Island (West Berkshire Playhouse) and Associate Lighting Designer for The Pillowman (National Theatre and tour). She was resident Lighting Designer at The Palace Theatre, Southend for some time and has an MSc in Light and Lighting.

Bindya Solanki Frehia/Officer Davis

Television credits include Nita in EastEnders (BBC), Dream Team (Sky 1), Sweet Revenge (BBC) and My Parents Are Aliens (Granada). She has also appeared in EastEnders Revealed, Network East Late, Children In Need, Sport Relief and Comic Relief. Theatre credits include Pramila in the tour of Deranged Marriage (Rifco), Juliet in Romeo And Juliet (English Shakespeare Company), Princess Jasmine in Aladdin (The Playhouse Weston-super-Mare), Skin Into Rainbows (Theatre Centre), The Magic Box (Tricycle Theatre), Eclipse… A Tale For Winter (Half Moon Theatre), Amrita in Monkey in the Stars, Stardog in Stardog Returns (Polka Theatre), Can You Kick It (Caught In The Act) and Arrange That Marriage (Watermans Arts Centre). Other recent work includes the radio production Dr Who And The Juggernauts, a promo for NTL and play readings for Kali Theatre. Bindya also co-hosted the Respect Festival at the Millennium Dome.

Lynne Verrall Jean

Theatre credits include House & Garden (Northampton); The Price (Octagon Theatre); Celaine (Hampstead); Entertaining Mr Sloane, Equus, Afore Night Come (Theatr Clwyd); Pale Horse (Royal Court); Dear Nobody (New Vic); Blue Night in the Heart of the West (Plain Clothes Productions – Bush, Traverse and tour), The Colony Comes a Cropper (Monstrous Regiment – BAC and tour); Mill Fire (Bush production at The Riverside); Everything in the Garden (Palace Theatre, Watford), My Dad's A' Nero, Duet for One (Derby Playhouse); Theory for the Attention of Mr Einstein (Old Red Lion); Coming Up (Belt & Braces, Half Moon and tour); Balls, My Girl (Warehouse, Croydon). Television work includes The Day that Britain Stopped; Holby City; Auf Wiedersen Pet; The Secret Life of Michael Fry; Doctors; Staying Alive (two series); Pretending to be Judith; Hetty Wainthrop Investigates; Casualty; Final Cut; Into the Fire; Precious Bane; House of Eliot; Inspector Morse; Hard Cases; The Bill; EastEnders; Fallen Sons; Childs Play; Peak Practice; Bill Brand; Starting Out. Film credits include New Town Original; A Kind of Hush and Elphida. Radio work includes Party Animal, Hotel du Lac and Biological Radio.

MERCY FINE

First published in 2005 by Oberon Books Ltd
521 Caledonian Road, London N7 9RH
Tel: +44 (0) 20 7607 3637 / Fax: +44 (0) 20 7607 3629
e-mail: info@oberonbooks.com
www.oberonbooks.com

A catalogue record for this book is available from the British
Library.

ISBN: 978-1-84002-637-5

Cover design by Frolic Design

Visit www.oberonbooks.com to read more about all our books
and to buy them. You will also find features, author interviews and
news of any author events, and you can sign up for e-newsletters
so that you're always first to hear about our new releases.

Characters

MERCY FINE

VIV WALKER

JEAN FINE

FREHIA ANDREWS

OFFICER DAVIS

1

To one side of the stage is a Formica table, set at all times with four chairs around it. The chairs should not match each other. An old fashioned armchair is beside the table. A man's pair of black work-boots are under one of the chairs. The laces are open, and each boot has one of a pair of socks hung over it. The boots are polished. A tabloid newspaper is on the table, open at the sports pages or page three.

Night. Dark. The door to the dormitory is open. MERCY FINE sits up in bed. A torch is shone in MERCY's face by OFFICER DAVIS who wears a red Santa hat with a bell on the end. There's a packet of pear drops under MERCY's pillow. OFFICER DAVIS enters and shines her torch at MERCY.

OFFICER DAVIS: Mercy Fine, why are you awake?

MERCY: Can't sleep, Miss Davis.

OFFICER DAVIS: Won't sleep?

MERCY: Can't sleep.

OFFICER DAVIS: Want some help?

MERCY: No.

OFFICER DAVIS: You sure?

MERCY: Don't want any help.

OFFICER DAVIS: I can get you some pills.

MERCY: Don't want any pills.

    Beat.

OFFICER DAVIS: You're too excited.

MERCY: Nervous.

OFFICER DAVIS: There's a lot to be nervous about. (*Beat.*) There's not a lot to be excited about.

MERCY: Thanks.

OFFICER DAVIS: All those people.

MERCY: All right…

OFFICER DAVIS: And you. How you going to cope Mercy Fine?

MERCY: I'll cope, Miss Davis.

OFFICER DAVIS: You'd better get some sleep then.

MERCY: Can't.

OFFICER DAVIS: You'll have bags.

MERCY: Then I'll carry them.

OFFICER DAVIS: You won't look beautiful.

MERCY: Beauty's in the eye of the beholder, Miss Davis.

OFFICER DAVIS: What's that supposed to mean?

Beat.

MERCY: That beauty is in the eye of the beholder. (*Beat.*) Miss Davis.

The flashlight is trailed around the room.

Why do you have to do that?

OFFICER DAVIS: What?

MERCY: Shine that bloody light in our faces.

OFFICER DAVIS: I'm making sure you're all tucked up. (*Beat.*) I'm off tomorrow.

MERCY: That's a shame.

OFFICER DAVIS: Miss me will you?

MERCY: Course I will.

OFFICER DAVIS: Have a good Christmas, Mercy Fine. Hope Santa brings you something nice. (*Beat.*) Mind if I…?

MERCY: Help yourself.

OFFICER DAVIS takes one pear drop, puts it in her mouth, then takes the whole packet.

Beat.

OFFICER DAVIS: Well, it is the season to give.

MERCY: And take.

OFFICER DAVIS: Where's your festive spirit?

Beat.

MERCY: (*Dead straight.*) Ho Ho Ho.

OFFICER DAVIS switches off the flashlight and exits the room. MERCY lies still. Eventually she sits up and switches on a small light by her bed.

Voices from around the room tell her: 'Sshhh.' 'Quiet Mercy.' 'Go to sleep.'

I can't.

A light comes on from VIV's bed.

VIV: Mercy!

MERCY: Sorry.

VIV: Why does she have to do that? Like we're going anywhere. It's just not on.

MERCY: And she nicked my pear drops.

VIV: Cow.

Beat.

VIV looks at her wristwatch.

It's gone midnight, Mercy.

MERCY: I wanted to stay awake until we slipped into a new day.

VIV: Well it's a new day now, so if you can't sleep, lie quietly.

MERCY: My adrenalin's going round, like a racing-car speeding through my veins.

VIV: Well you're a driver, park it for the night.

MERCY: What?

VIV: Park it? I mean metaphorically. You know. Metaphors and similes.

MERCY: Yeah.

A collective 'sshhh' from the other beds.

VIV: In twenty-four hours you'll be home.

MERCY: Yeah.

VIV: In your own bed.

MERCY: Not mine.

VIV: It won't be prison property.

MERCY: Suppose not.

VIV: Wish it was me. Now go to sleep.

Beat.

MERCY: Bit more than twenty-four.

VIV switches on her light again. There is a low moan from another bed.

VIV: What?

MERCY: More like thirty-two. If you count from now until I actually go.

VIV: *Oh merde! Près de vingt-quatre heures.*

MERCY: What?

VIV: Have you forgotten everything I taught you?

MERCY: *Mais non.* (*Beat.*) I've been waiting for this moment for nine years, three months, two weeks, two days and thirty-two hours.

VIV: Yeah well. Don't spoil it. Remember it.

MERCY: Remember it?

VIV: So you can tell your grandchildren.

MERCY: Like I'll ever forget it. (*Beat.*) You have to have kids before you can have grand-kids.

VIV: You can have mine. Now go to sleep.

MERCY: Viv!

VIV: What?

Beat.

MERCY: I don't want to go.

VIV: To sleep? Yeah, you said.

MERCY: I don't want to go. Tomorrow.

VIV: You don't want to leave?

MERCY: Can't. Not ready.

VIV: Try and get some sleep. Everything will seem better in the morning.

Beat.

MERCY: Tell me a story.

VIV: Now?

MERCY: You know, once upon a time…beginning, middle, end.

VIV: I know what a story is. I'll wake the others up.

MERCY: No you won't. Not if you sit here. (*She points to her bed.*)

VIV: What do you think I am?

MERCY: My teacher. You're my teacher.

VIV: All right then. But only a short one. Then sleep. What would you like? Austen? Dickens? Or some Martina Cole?

MERCY: I like the ones you make-up best. But only the middle bit. I don't want the beginning. And I definitely do not want the end.

VIV: Not that again.

MERCY: Please. I like the middle.

VIV gets out of her bed and sits on the edge of MERCY's bed.

VIV: Lie back. Close your eyes.

MERCY leaves her eyes open.

I said close them.

MERCY: They are closed. Metaphorically.

VIV: Sshhh. (*Pause.*) Now, the girl's eyes opened wide at the sight in front of her. She'd never seen anything quite like it…

Lights fade on VIV and MERCY.

2

The lights come up on JEAN. She stands by the Formica table, and dips a sponge into a bowl of water, squeezes it, then cleans the table meticulously for a few moments. JEAN should have a handbag, with make-up in it and bright coloured lipstick.

JEAN: I want it to be clean. Clean for when my girl comes home. This table means a lot to her. She loves this table. It has memories. Stories. Fairy stories and romantic stories. Good stories and bad stories. But I don't like the bad ones. I don't like them.

JEAN dips the sponge into the water and squeezes, then cleans again. She stops momentarily and stares at a mark on the table. She smoothes her hands across it and stops.

This is where her father sliced through a loaf of bread. He didn't listen to me, just slammed it down and cut. And cut. Cut right through the table. He said he didn't like breadboards, didn't see the point. The table was for everything. So he sliced right into it. (*Pause.*) When Frank came he made different marks. There. And there. Every cut on this table's got a story. She knows the stories. (*Beat.*) And I know the stories.

JEAN leaves the sponge on the table, and sits behind the table.

3

The Drawing Room. Morning. Outside, the trees are bare. The fireplace is blocked up. Christmas decorations are in a box, some spilling out. VIV is doing The Times crossword. Lightning dances across the room. FREHIA stands facing the wall, practising dance moves. She has a roll-up behind

her ear. Rolled up on the floor, is a yoga mat. FREHIA
waits for the thunder.

FREHIA: One, two, three, four, five, six…

A rumble of thunder fills the room.

It's getting closer.

VIV: What is?

FREHIA: The thunder. (*Beat.*) Which is more than I can
say for your parole. (*Beat.*) I like thunder. It's exciting.
Do you like thunder, Viv?

VIV: Just a minute…

FREHIA: Do you think she's coming?

VIV: Hold on a minute, Frehia.

VIV adds another answer to the crossword.

FREHIA: We gotta leave soon.

VIV: Hold on.

FREHIA: We gotta leave and I gotta have a smoke. You
gonna talk to me?

VIV finishes her crossword.

VIV: Yes. Just…one…minute…there.

VIV puts down the newspaper.

What did you say?

Beat.

FREHIA: I gotta have a smoke.

VIV: I didn't think you were supposed to smoke?

FREHIA: I pray then I smoke. Works for me.

FREHIA moves to her rolled up yoga mat excitedly. She unrolls it and stands beside it, smiling.

Well?

VIV: Well what?

FREHIA: What do you think?

VIV: About what?

FREHIA: My yoga mat which also doubles up as a prayer mat.

VIV: Isn't that blasphemous?

FREHIA: I'm not saying anything rude about it. It just means it has a two-in-one function. I'm gonna sell them when I get out. Spell it 'yoger mat' – you know, Y – O – G – E – R – as in yoga and prayer…

VIV: Really.

FREHIA: Yeah.

VIV: And who do you think will buy this yoger mat?

FREHIA: People who pray. And do yoga. I'm gonna make my fortune.

VIV: There are plenty of other ways to do that.

FREHIA: You should know.

VIV glares at FREHIA.

What's it say, in the papers?

VIV: Usual. Depressing world we live in. Sometimes I think we're safer in here than out there.

FREHIA: Guess what I've asked Santa for this year?

VIV: Hasn't anyone told you Santa isn't real?

FREHIA: Yeah he is. Guess what I've asked for?

VIV: Surprise me.

FREHIA: Actually, if I tell you I won't get it. (*Beat.*) Come on Mercy. (*Beat.*) Will you listen to my song? For Mercy.

VIV: Do I have to?

FREHIA: Yeah. It's a surprise.

VIV: I'm sure it will be.

FREHIA: It's my Christmas treat.

VIV: I've got things to do.

FREHIA: What things?

VIV: Work. I'm expecting a delivery of books.

FREHIA: You call sitting in a room all day surrounded by books, work.

VIV: It's what I know.

FREHIA: So, my song.

VIV: Go on then.

> *FREHIA stands centre-stage.*

FREHIA: Right. If I could have music I would.

VIV: Mercy doesn't like music.

FREHIA: You have to imagine me on the stage at Bert's Hall.

VIV: Where?

FREHIA: My brother always call it Bert's Hall.

VIV: Oh!

FREHIA: So. Here we go. (*Beat.*) I'm nervous now.

VIV: Just get on with it.

FREHIA: Okay okay. (*Pause.*) 'Fill the decks with boughs of holly. Holly. Holly. Fill the decks with boughs of holly. Fa la la la la la la la la.'

VIV: It's deck the halls.

FREHIA: What?

VIV: It's 'deck the halls with boughs of holly'.

FREHIA: Oh. Right. Thanks.

VIV: Is that it?

FREHIA: No, there's more.

VIV: Later. Has the food been taken care of?

FREHIA: Yeah.

VIV: Who's making the cake? Tish is good at baking. I used to bake you know.

FREHIA: No one's making it.

VIV: Why not?

FREHIA: Gov said we had to buy it. We can't use prison resources on a cake. I said buying one's using prison resources. He said if you do for one you have to do for all. So I said do for all then. (*Beat.*) He didn't like that either.

VIV: Don't tell her about the cake.

FREHIA: I won't.

VIV: So where are you two working today?

FREHIA: Charity shop.

VIV: You know what they say.

FREHIA: Charity begins at home. (*Beat.*) Someone else's.

MERCY enters. FREHIA rolls up her yoga mat.

Where have you been? We'll be late.

MERCY: No we won't.

FREHIA: Don't want to be late on your last day.

MERCY: We won't be late. I've been welcoming the new girl. Debbie.

VIV: Did you tell her to watch out for Miss Davis?

MERCY: Yeah. (*Beat.*) She seems okay. Bit scared of thunder.

FREHIA: Pussy girl.

MERCY: Don't you give her a hard time.

FREHIA: Me? (*Meaning VIV.*) She's the one you want to worry about. (*Beat.*) You ready then?

MERCY: Yeah.

VIV: You all packed?

MERCY shrugs.

FREHIA: It's like you're going on holiday.

VIV: What time will you be back?

MERCY: Usual time.

VIV: Okay. I'll see if I can get the Governor to give us a bottle of something nice to send you off with.

FREHIA: Chardonnay?

VIV: Diet Coke.

FREHIA: (*Exiting.*) I'm outside having a smoke.

FREHIA exits with her yoga mat under her arm as she removes the roll-up from behind her ear ready to light.

MERCY: Why's she taken her yoga mat with her?

VIV: It's become her comfort blanket. And God knows
sometimes she needs comforting.

MERCY: Thanks for reading to me last night.

VIV: It's okay. Feel any different today?

MERCY shakes her head.

Still want to stay?

MERCY: I didn't want to get out of bed this morning.

VIV: I know. I saw you.

MERCY: You're around later, yeah?

VIV: I thought I'd go into London, do some shopping,
have lunch then take the Eurostar to Paris for the night.
Of course I'm around.

MERCY: Good. Better go. Charity awaits us.

*MERCY exits. VIV puts up the decorations. She puts them
all up, and when she's finished, she exits.*

4

Lights up on JEAN.

JEAN: I sit here. (*Pointing opposite her.*) And Frank sits over
there. And my girl sits in the middle, like the middle
of a story. She is the bit everyone listens to. And this
seat…this seat is reserved for visitors. But we don't get
many of them. The gasman. The electric man. The odd
Christian wanting to pray for my soul. (*Beat.*) Lord have
mercy on my soul. (*Pause.*) Mercy says, 'Mum, keep it
for me. I don't want anything else, just this table.' So
I do. I keep it clean for her. No one wants to eat off a

dirty table. He doesn't like eating off a dirty table. He doesn't like it.

The lights fade on JEAN.

5

MERCY and FREHIA are sitting in the car; MERCY's at the wheel. MERCY has a bag. One or two expletives from FREHIA along the way wouldn't go amiss.

FREHIA: Is this too cold for you?

MERCY: No.

FREHIA: Can I put the radio on?

MERCY: I like to drive in silence.

FREHIA: (*Singing.*) Silent night…You'll be able to drive all alone soon in your own car. (*Beat.*) What about talking? Can I talk?

MERCY: Silence is better.

FREHIA: You sure you're not cold? I can close the window if you are.

MERCY: I like it. When the wind hits my face, it's the best feeling in the world. It's as near as I'll get to being kissed.

FREHIA: All right.

MERCY: As near as I'll get to being made love to, having someone spoil me. Not that anyone ever spoiled me before. My dad, yeah, he would buy me sweets but it's not the same.

FREHIA: I like aniseed balls. Send us some when you're out?

MERCY: All right.

FREHIA: You won't.

MERCY: I might.

FREHIA: You won't. No one ever does.

MERCY: Well I'm different.

FREHIA: Yeah you are. Can I drive on the way back?

MERCY: You mad?

FREHIA: Won't tell.

MERCY: How many points you got now?

FREHIA: Loads.

MERCY: Sorry, but no. Pills and points are not a good combination.

FREHIA: You don't seem very excited about your parole. (*Beat.*) Who's coming to get you in the morning?

MERCY: No one.

FREHIA: Oh, that's a shame. Maybe you can drive yourself to the station.

MERCY: Maybe I'll walk.

FREHIA: It's too cold. (*Beat.*) What about your mum? She could come and get you.

MERCY: She doesn't drive.

FREHIA: She could get a taxi. Come pick you up. Maybe she's made you some nice food.

MERCY: She doesn't cook any more.

FREHIA: I want to taste the food cooked from my mother's hands. She has the most beautiful hands, you know.

MERCY: My mother has small hands, and short nails, no nails really, bitten down, right down, so the edges bleed. Sometimes, if she let them grow, she'd let me do them. We'd sit by the kitchen table and she'd smile and look into my eyes as I soaked her hands and buffed and filed. And made her pretty. She was pretty, Frehia.

FREHIA: And what is she now, an ugly cow?

FREHIA laughs.

MERCY: Don't say that.

Beat.

FREHIA: We'll look pretty tonight.

MERCY: Will we?

FREHIA: Yeah. And we'll have fun. Quite a few of the girls are coming.

MERCY: Where?

FREHIA: (*Realising what's she just said.*) Err....nothing. I mean coming to the dining-room. To eat. With you. Last supper kind of thing. Only you're not going to die.

MERCY: That's all right then. (*Beat.*) You just said something you shouldn't have?

FREHIA: No.

MERCY: Don't worry, I won't let on I know.

FREHIA: There's nothing to know. Shit!

MERCY: Do me a favour, have a look in my bag. Might be a couple of sweets hiding in there.

FREHIA: You're not supposed to eat in here.

MERCY: Well we better not tell anyone then.

FREHIA: You know, sometimes you're really wicked.

FREHIA opens MERCY's bag, and removes a bag of sweets. FREHIA offers the bag to MERCY. She takes a sweet.

MERCY: Thank you. My mum always taught me that manners maketh man. So now, whenever anyone says anything nasty to me, when they call me names, I just say thank you. They can't reply to that.

FREHIA: You ain't evil. Just human. That's the thing. They all think we're different, like we were born with something different, but we ain't. We're just like everyone else.

MERCY: I've been thinking about it all. The before and the after. But I've got to find a way to move forwards, move on.

FREHIA: You should have French lessons when you get out.

MERCY: Viv's been great.

FREHIA: Proper French lessons.

MERCY: *Je suis une femme.*

FREHIA: *Oui.*

MERCY: I'll miss Viv.

FREHIA: What about me?

Beat.

Will you miss me?

Beat.

Will you miss me, Mercy Fine?

Beat.

MERCY: Course I will.

Beat.

FREHIA: You must be feeling fucking fantastic. The world is your oyster.

MERCY: Not yet.

FREHIA: Tomorrow your life changes. You'll be a free person.

MERCY: Stop going on about it. I'm nervous enough as it is.

FREHIA: There's a lot to be nervous about. It's a jungle out there. There's lions and tigers and even leopards. Scares the shit out of me when I go home. There's so many people and strange faces all looking at you, like they know.

MERCY: Please, could you just shut up.

FREHIA takes another sweet and sits silently. She crunches loudly on a sweet, looks apologetically at MERCY.

6

Lights fade and come up on JEAN, who is sitting by the table.

JEAN: I'm making her favourite food. Spicy potatoes. She's got a good appetite, my girl. Just like her father. She looks like him too. My girl. She has his eyes. My girl. My Mercy. Lord have mercy on her soul. But what about mine? What about my soul?

JEAN starts to clean the table again.

7

MERCY rushes on energetically with FREHIA behind her. They stop by a door. There's a larger than life sign above it in almost surreal letters, which reads 'GOVERNOR SMITH'.

MERCY: Fuck, fuck, fuck. Just go will you.

FREHIA: I want to help.

MERCY: You can't help. Just go.

FREHIA: What you gonna do, Mercy?

MERCY: Tell him what happened.

FREHIA: Yeah. That's good. Tell him what happened. Tell him it was an accident. You were provoked. Yeah, provoked.

MERCY: Piss off will you Frehia.

FREHIA: That's nice. I only want to help. I was there. I saw it.

MERCY: Yeah, you and everyone else. Glaring at me like I'm some specimen.

FREHIA: It's no big deal. It ain't a crime.

MERCY: Anything I do is a crime. You don't get it do you?

FREHIA: I got words Mercy Fine. They may not always be the right words, but I got them. And I got eyes.

MERCY: And who do you think they're going to believe? The eyes and ears of a good girl, or the eyes and ear of a bad one?

FREHIA: I ain't bad. I like the juice too much, that's all. And sometimes I mix my juice. And sometimes I get behind the wheel of someone else's car and let the juice take over.

MERCY: One day you'll kill someone.

FREHIA: Like you did?

Pause.

Let me come with you.

MERCY: You just don't know when to stop.

FREHIA: It slipped out.

MERCY: Viv's the only one who keeps her mouth shut.
    All the time I've been in here, she's never once asked
    me why I'm here.

FREHIA: But she knows.

MERCY: She's never asked me.

FREHIA: Is that why you're friends? Is that why you tell
    her everything?

MERCY: Not everything.

FREHIA: I keep my mouth shut.

MERCY: You? No one ever knows what's going to come
    out of your mouth.

FREHIA: They call me spontaneous. (*Beat.*) Come on.
    Let's practice what you're gonna say. Like rôle-playing.

MERCY: I'm not an actor.

FREHIA: Yeah you are. We all are. You, me, Viv's the
    biggest actor of the lot.

    *MERCY shakes her head like she can't believe what she's
    about to do. FREHIA coughs. When she speaks her voice is
    lower than usual.*

    Mercy Fine. What have you done?

MERCY: I'm not doing it if you put on an idiot's voice.

    FREHIA does her usual voice.

FREHIA: It's Governor Smith.

MERCY: That is not Governor Smith. And if he hears you
    doing that you'll get your privileges taken away. Hurry up.

FREHIA: What happened?

MERCY: It was an accident.

FREHIA: An accident?

MERCY: Yeah.

FREHIA: Governor Smith…

MERCY: Governor Smith.

FREHIA: Tell me what occurred?

MERCY: Occurred? What kind of word is that?

FREHIA: That's what he'd say. Occurred. He likes to feel clever.

MERCY: Well, sir, what occurred, was this. We were walking to the shop.

FREHIA: Which shop?

MERCY: You know which shop.

FREHIA: I do. But Governor Smith doesn't.

MERCY: The charity shop.

FREHIA: Which charity?

MERCY: Frehia!

FREHIA: Governor Smith is into details.

MERCY: Geranium shop. For the blind.

FREHIA: I see. (*Beat.*) What were you doing?

MERCY: I'd just parked the car. (*Beat.*) I'd just parked the car, and we were walking to the shop.

FREHIA: Was that girl there?

MERCY: Which girl?

FREHIA: The pretty one.

MERCY can't think who the pretty girl is.

Frehia Andrews.

MERCY: Yes, she was there.

FREHIA: She's one of the good ones you know.

MERCY: Really.

FREHIA: Yeah. Since she converted, well, she's changed.

MERCY: But she still drinks. And drives. What do you think of that Governor Smith?

FREHIA: Hey, I'll ask the questions.

MERCY: Frehia, this is about me, not you. If you want to help me, fine, if not, go and annoy someone else.

FREHIA: Tell me what happened.

MERCY: We were walking to the shop. This woman comes up to me, from nowhere, and she looks at me. Stares at me.

Beat.

FREHIA: Then what?

MERCY: She calls me a fucking coon.

FREHIA: And?

MERCY: She spits in my face.

FREHIA: What did you do?

MERCY: I spat back. I couldn't help it.

FREHIA: What you did was wrong.

MERCY: I know.

FREHIA: And if someone from the shop hadn't told us, were you going to?

MERCY: Of course. (*Beat.*) The thing is, if I didn't do that, I might have…punched her.

FREHIA: Don't say that.

MERCY: And I was never violent before coming here.

FREHIA: You killed someone before coming here. (*Beat.*) It wasn't me saying that, it was Governor Smith. (*Beat.*) Haven't we taught you anything Mercy Fine?

MERCY: You've taught me how to be angry and pissed off and hateful. You put us lot together and sometimes, you bring out the worst in us. You're meant to prepare us for the world, but you prepare us for shit. You know that? You prepare us for shit. You send us to anger management and you know what, I come out feeling more angry than when I went in. And I am not an angry person.

VOICE: (*Off.*) Mercy Fine.

FREHIA: Don't say that.

The door opens. FREHIA and MERCY look at it. MERCY composes herself.

MERCY looks at FREHIA and enters the room. The door closes. FREHIA waits a moment, puts her ear to the door, then looks slowly over her shoulder as if she realises she's being watched, and she smiles and walks away. Lights fade.

8

JEAN sits at the table.

JEAN: He brought me flowers. A dozen red roses. Long stemmed. Four pounds each. I was worth it. (*Beat.*) He loved me. And I loved him. I loved him. (*Beat.*) He brought her chocolate. Dark chocolate. (*Beat.*) Under the dark there's always light. Under the dark there's always…

9

Lights come up on MERCY. She is outside, sitting on the ground, head in her hands.

VIV: What did he say?

MERCY takes her time.

MERCY: They might keep me in.

VIV: They can't.

MERCY: I told him, when he decides what he wants to do, he should come and find me and let me go. Or keep me here. But he has to come and tell me. He can't let me wait until the morning.

VIV: They can't keep you in.

MERCY: They can do what they want. I caused a member of the public harm.

VIV: So he just expects you to wait?

MERCY: He said maybe I need longer to learn my lesson. I can't go round spitting at someone just because they spit at me.

VIV: He's worried about his reputation.

MERCY: What about mine? (*Beat.*) I'm lucky she didn't press charges.

VIV: It isn't a crime.

MERCY: He said in some places it is and I was lucky I wasn't in some places.

VIV: Maybe the woman who spat in your face should be given a bed in here for the night.

MERCY: Yeah.

VIV: In a room with thirteen others. With their smells and moods. Then let's see how she feels.

MERCY: I said, what's the difference between her and me? He said, she didn't do what I've done. (*Beat.*) Will no one ever let me forget? They were going to let me drive myself to the station in the morning. But now they don't think it would be such a good idea. They don't want to give the public the wrong impression. They need to protect them.

VIV: The public? The public? We are the public.

MERCY: He says I have a disorder.

VIV: What kind of disorder?

MERCY: Personality disorder.

VIV: We've all got one of those. There is absolutely nothing wrong with you.

MERCY: Maybe there is. He said, 'Mercy Fine, if I have my way, I'll send you back to a closed prison for six months at the least. We've been good to you, we've given you a chance, even got you a job. We're trying to set you up in the world. But if this is what you're like here, what will you be like out there?' (*Beat.*) He always gets his way.

VIV: Not always.

MERCY: They're having a meeting.

VIV: When?

MERCY: Now.

VIV: Them and their bloody meetings. They'll have meetings to shit soon. (*Beat.*) What did I tell you? Don't let them get into here, into this. (*Meaning her head.*) Once they get in here you're finished. Look at you. When you were transferred here, you were bright and excited and hopeful. The model prisoner. You never question anything. And now this.

MERCY: I did wrong, Viv.

VIV: You did not do wrong.

MERCY: I spat at someone.

VIV: You did what anyone else would have done.

MERCY: Would you?

VIV: No. I'd have punched her.

MERCY: But I shouldn't have spat at her.

VIV: She shouldn't have done it to you. Treat a person like a dog and they'll bark.

MERCY: Woof!

MERCY laughs.

Woof, woof!

VIV: Come on.

MERCY: I want to stay out here.

VIV: You'll feel better tomorrow. (*Beat.*) You're going home.

MERCY: He's gonna keep me in.

MERCY laughs.

VIV: What's so funny?

MERCY: I said I wanted to stay. Last night I said I didn't want to go. And now…I might just get what I wanted.

VOICE: (*Tannoy.*) You'll be pleased to know your post is ready for collection at the central desk.

VIV exits.

10

Lights up on JEAN.

JEAN: Pass the bread please, Frank. (*Beat.*) I said please. (*Louder and with more integrity.*) Please. (*She takes the bread.*) Thank you. (*She looks scared, as if being threatened.*) Don't say that. I said please don't say that, Frank. (*Beat.*) Because it's not nice. Because it hurts. (*Beat.*) (*Then quietly.*) Sticks and stones. Sticks and stones. Sorry. (*Louder.*) Sorry. (*Louder still.*) I said sorry. (*Pause.*) I made it today. Especially for you. It's a pie. (*Beat.*) Your favourite. (*Beat.*) Because you said, you said you liked… (*Beat.*) I'm lazy. (*Beat.*) I'm lazy. (*Beat.*) I'm a lazy cow. (*Beat.*) I'm an ugly cow. (*Beat.*) I'm wearing make-up. Here. And here.

JEAN applies lipstick.

Where are you going? (*Beat.*) Will you be long? (*Beat.*) No. No. It's fine. You stay out as long as you want. (*Beat.*) Yes. I'll be here.

Offstage a door bangs. JEAN stays still, and waits a moment, and then she cries, into herself, very held in.

Sticks and stones. Sticks and stones.

11

Outside. Lights up. VIV stands beside MERCY. VIV holds a letter.

MERCY: Who's it from?

VIV: Ron.

MERCY: Sending more money? Topping up your account.

VIV: Come inside?

MERCY shakes her head. Beat.

MERCY: Why are you my friend?

VIV: I like you.

MERCY: I make you feel good do I?

VIV: No.

MERCY: I make you feel good about yourself do I?

VIV: I said no.

MERCY shakes her head.

You know, you could take control of things. Instead of giving in. You could go in there now, speak to Governor Smith, apologise, tell him the last thing you expected was a stranger calling you names and spitting at you. Tell him it's what you fear most when you get out. Take control, Mercy.

MERCY: Or what?

VIV: Or do nothing. Go back to a closed prison, in a cell alone with no charity work and no driving. Imagine that. No driving. It's what you live for isn't it? Getting out there, in your car. It's what you love.

MERCY ignores VIV. VIV exits. MERCY sits looking out, just looking.

12

JEAN gets up and walks to the table. All the while the sun is gradually setting, it's getting darker outside. JEAN opens the drawer and removes a tied-up cloth which has something in it, and places it on the table. She undoes the cloth, and reveals the shattered pieces of blue and white china plates. She tries to fit them together, but when she realises this is impossible, she puts them back in the cloth and goes back to her seat.

13

VIV is standing over MERCY, holding the green apple out to her.

VIV: We missed you at dinner.

MERCY: Not hungry. (*Beat.*) Teacher's pet. They'll call me teacher's pet. That apple makes me think of him.

VIV: What?

MERCY: Standing in the kitchen, offering it to me, like you are now. Calling me names.

VIV: Who called you names?

MERCY: He did. My mum's man. (*Beat.*) Frank.

Beat.

VIV: You never said.

MERCY: You never asked.

VIV: You should have said.

MERCY: They're not the kind of words you want to say.

VIV puts the apple in her pocket.

Have I been out here long?

VIV: Two hours. Tish said you were still here.

MERCY: What about roll check?

VIV: I explained.

MERCY: Why'd you do that?

VIV: Because they listen to me.

MERCY: Why do they listen to you?

VIV: Because they do.

MERCY: Because you're posh.

VIV: I'm not.

MERCY: I never thought I'd have a posh friend.

VIV: I never thought I'd have a…

MERCY: What? (*Beat.*) Is that what excited you? Being close to someone like me? So you can tell all your friends. You were friends with Mercy Fine.

VIV: No.

MERCY: You can have a good gossip, say you were there. You touched evil. Or is it because I make you feel superior?

VIV: For God's sake Mercy. If all this is just because you don't want to leave prison, then say so.

MERCY: I already said so.

VIV: Fine. Then stay here forever. It's your life.

Pause.

MERCY: I'm scared.

VIV: Me too.

MERCY: I'm scared of out there.

VIV: We're all scared.

MERCY: Not you.

VIV: Yes, me.

MERCY: What you scared of?

VIV: That I'll get out of prison and fuck up again. That Ron will leave me.

MERCY: How is Ron?

VIV: He's off with one of his girls on a winter cruise.

MERCY: One of his girls?

VIV: New season new girl. Oh, it's okay, I mean I can't expect him to keep his dick to himself while I'm in here.

MERCY: But you're home every few weeks.

VIV: Poor love. If his tackle doesn't get a bite twice a day, well, it thinks its blood supply's been cut. We came to an agreement. I said as long as you're safe. And please spare me the details.

MERCY: What about your kids?

VIV: What about them?

Beat.

MERCY: You got sad eyes, Viv. *Votre yeux sont…*sad.

VIV: Triste.

MERCY: Triste.

Beat.

VIV: What do you want to do?

MERCY: Stay out here. Watch the moon. Feel the moon on my skin.

VIV: Okay.

VIV starts to exit.

MERCY: Don't go. (*Beat.*) Please.

VIV stays where she is.

I don't want to go home.

VIV: You said.

MERCY: I don't want to see her.

VIV: Who?

MERCY: My mum.

VIV: She'll want to see you. She hasn't been here for a while, has she?

Beat.

MERCY: She's never been. Not here. Not in the last three prisons I've been in. (*Beat.*) She was coming, once. The first time. Just after I'd been... She was coming then. When I was sharing with two and queuing for a piss. I was going to have a whole twenty minutes with her. I got changed. Put on my best clothes. Combed my hair. Brushed my teeth. They said she was coming. They said she'd be here. She's a good timekeeper. But when the time came, she didn't come. I was worried about her. Maybe she'd had an accident. She never came.

VIV: I don't know what to say.

MERCY: There there it'll be all right.

VIV: There there it'll be all right.

MERCY: It fucking won't.

VIV looks at her watch.

What you got to do that's so urgent?

VIV: Things.

MERCY: What things?

VIV: Just things.

MERCY: Am I ruining it?

VIV: What?

MERCY: My party?

VIV: What party?

MERCY: It's all right. I don't like surprises anyway.

VIV: Did Frehia tell you?

MERCY: No.

VIV: Then who?

MERCY: I guessed.

VIV: She told you. The little sod.

MERCY: You can cancel.

VIV: No I won't.

MERCY: Because I'm not in the mood for a party. And there's probably nothing to celebrate because I'm not getting out.

VIV: You're leaving here in the morning and we're giving you a send off, whether you like it or not. They can't keep you in.

MERCY: Of course they can.

VIV: It's power, that's all. He wants to keep you in your place until he has no more power over you. That's all it is.

MERCY: It's not like I've got anywhere to go.

VIV: You have a home.

MERCY: A room in a hostel.

VIV: Right now, Mercy, it all seems impossible. And it's so much easier for you to fuck up and stay inside. Don't do it. Don't fuck up. Be brave. Be scared. Be excited. But don't fuck up.

Pause.

MERCY: Do me a favour.

VIV: Depends.

MERCY: Ask the Governor if I can see him?

VIV nods and exits.

14

Lights up on JEAN. She cleans the table. She stops when she comes to a mark on the table.

JEAN: She was twelve when I caught her smoking. Sitting here. She got such a fright when she saw me, she tried to put it out on the table. I said, don't smoke. Don't smoke Mercy. It's bad for you.

JEAN cleans again.

I've got to clean. I've got to make it nice.

JEAN stops cleaning.

15

The sign that reads 'GOVERNOR SMITH' is lit again. The door is open. MERCY stands centre-stage, looking out. She is waiting. Under MERCY, JEAN speaks, softly, almost inaudibly. A clock ticks in the background.

MERCY: I didn't do it on purpose. It was wrong, I know, but I was provoked. In a way it was good that it happened while I was here, because I could see what I'll face in the outside world. It was a mistake. A big mistake. It scared me, because it made me realise that we all have it in us to harm others. Only I never want to harm anyone. I accept that I did wrong. Don't keep me in. Please.

JEAN: Lord have mercy on my soul. Lord have mercy on my soul. Lord have mercy on my soul. Lord have mercy on my soul.

Lights fade on MERCY and remain on JEAN as she cleans the table.

16

The Drawing Room. The room has been decorated with Christmas decorations. MERCY enters.

VIV: What did he say?

MERCY: Nothing.

VIV: He must have said something.

MERCY: He timed me.

VIV: What for?

MERCY: He gave me sixty seconds to absolve myself.

VIV: And did you?

MERCY shrugs.

MERCY: I said I'd learned, I had moved on.

VIV: Well done Mercy, telling him what he wants to hear. Feed his ego, he'll let you go for that. He likes to think the system works.

MERCY: Sometimes it does.

VIV: Yeah, right. (*Beat.*) I bet he lets you go.

MERCY: I bet he keeps me in.

VIV: I wouldn't bet with me if I were you.

MERCY: Why, are you going to cheat?

VIV: You'll never know if I do. What do you want to bet me?

MERCY: If I win? Your Chanel. And you can have my pear drops.

VIV: That's not fair.

MERCY: Who said anything about fair?

VIV: You have learned something.

MERCY: Yeah, like I said to the Governor. (*Beat.*) Viv, do you ever think about not being here?

VIV: All the time.

MERCY: It'll be weird.

VIV: You'll get used to it. Just like you got used to being here.

MERCY: Who said I got used to it?

VIV: I did. (*Meaning: I got used to it.*)

MERCY: Ever since I've been inside, I've never stood under the moon at midnight.

VIV: I've never done that.

MERCY: I could just go out the back tonight, for a moment.

VIV: You can't do as you please yet.

MERCY: I hate rules.

VIV: They're made for breaking.

MERCY: Then let me break one.

VIV: You already did. Thou shalt not commit a crime when you've already committed one.

MERCY: I just want to feel the moon on my skin at midnight.

VIV: 'Want' doesn't come into it. Anyway, it's freezing. And the moon's probably behind a cloud, so you can forget about feeling it on your skin.

MERCY: But it'll be there. It's always there. Under the dark there is always light.

FREHIA enters with a Sainsbury's bag.

FREHIA: Mercy in here?

VIV: Can't you read?

FREHIA: Governor wants to see you.

MERCY: Okay.

FREHIA: He said now.

MERCY: And I said okay.

VIV: She'll be a second.

FREHIA: He's got a right face on him. What have you done now, Mercy Fine?

MERCY sighs and exits and stands outside the Governor's office. FREHIA looks around the room, at the decorations.

Nice one!

FREHIA removes a box from the plastic bag. It's a Spongebob Square Pants Happy Birthday cake.

VIV: What is it?

FREHIA: A cake.

VIV: What flavour?

FREHIA: Cake flavour.

VIV looks at the box.

VIV: A birthday cake?

FREHIA: I like Spongebob.

VIV: This isn't about you, Frehia.

FREHIA: It is her birthday, sort of. From tomorrow it'll be like she's reborn. Inshallah!

VIV: I hope she'll be all right.

FREHIA: She's fine. Governor's probably giving her a talk, you know, remember everything you've learned in here, remember to be an upstanding member of the community, remember that we care about you. Remember that this is a journey, and we're all on it together. We're in the driving seat, and you're a passenger, but when you leave here it's the other way around. Except Mercy is a driver, isn't she, she drives people around, so she's the driver. I don't drive any more. I'm driven. Remember, Mercy Fine, remember. Don't ever forget or you'll end up back in here.

VIV: How do you know all that?

FREHIA: Heard it last time I was in. (*Beat.*) And the time before. Sometimes, they give you a talk, a mini lecture. Makes them feel good. Makes them feel they've achieved something. Like they've done you this big fuck-off favour. But the last thing you want the night before you get out is some middle-aged bloke poking a finger at you, smiling and telling you how you should and shouldn't behave. Remember, remember, never forget or you'll be back. Society is on the lookout for your kind. Oh yeah, what's my kind?

VIV: Can you stop, for a moment? Just for a moment?

FREHIA: I know, I talk too much. I talk to everyone. All the time. I'm troubled. Disturbed. Juxtaposed. What is it they call me? Bi-polar. It's not my fault. It's just the way I was born. Some people are born good. Some people are born like me. Not good not bad. Just inconvenienced. It's in my genes, you know. You know, in here.

VIV: Have you taken your pills?

FREHIA: Pills…?

VIV: For God's sake take them. Before you talk us into tomorrow.

FREHIA exits and leaves the cake on the table. VIV looks at her watch.

17

The Dorm. MERCY is sitting on the side of her bed. By her feet is a suitcase, closed. JEAN is at the table. VIV stands on the threshold.

VIV: Mind if I come in?

MERCY: It's your room.

VIV: You look like you want a bit of peace and quiet.

MERCY: I'll have enough of that soon.

VIV: He's not sending you back to…

MERCY shrugs her head and smiles. VIV sighs, laughs, a nervous laugh.

MERCY: I'm getting out.

VIV: Yes! I win.

MERCY: I thought he'd keep me in, send me back to a closed prison. Test me, you know, see if I responded. If I argued. If I'd beg him to let me go. But I'm a good girl. I went in, sat down and listened.

VIV: Yeah, and…

MERCY: Remember, be good, stay out of trouble. Mercy Fine, you are a model prisoner. You have never said you were innocent, which means I have accepted my guilt. And it is only when we accept our guilt that we can move on. He said the incident today was isolated, and in a way, it was good it happened while I was still inside. Which is exactly what I'd said to him. He said, please do not go killing anyone else. And I laughed. And he ticked another fucking box. He had my release papers ready – he wished me luck, said he didn't want to see me in here again, and that was it.

VIV: Mercy Fine, model prisoner.

MERCY: That's me.

VIV: Great!

MERCY: You can have your party now.

VIV: Party, what party?

MERCY: Viv, I need to talk.

Beat.

VIV: What about?

MERCY: Stuff.

VIV: You've had four years.

MERCY: Yeah, well there's never been a right time.

VIV: Go on then.

Pause.

MERCY: I'm not sure how to start. Where to start.

VIV: You're not about to confess are you?

MERCY: It's not what you think.

VIV: Skeletons in the cupboard?

Beat.

MERCY: Drawing Room in five minutes?

VIV: Okay. (*Beat.*) I'm pleased you're going.

MERCY: Yeah, me too.

VIV exits. MERCY starts to pack, slowly at first, then with an energy like never before. Lights fade on MERCY.

18

The Drawing Room. Lights up on VIV rearranging the Christmas decorations. MERCY enters.

VIV: All packed?

MERCY: Yeah. Felt strange. Knowing I won't be unpacking that lot upstairs again. You done this?

VIV: Might have.

MERCY: For me?

VIV: For all of us.

MERCY: Posh!

VIV: Believe me, this is not posh.

MERCY: I bet you have crystal decorations on your tree at home.

VIV: Which one?

MERCY: You got more than one tree?

VIV: Two. Usually.

MERCY: Unusually. Fancy chocolates hanging off the branches?

VIV: Can't stand the stuff. Give me cheap chocolate any day. (*Beat.*) So?

MERCY: So?

VIV: Confession time. Go on then. Tell me.

MERCY: Not sure how to.

VIV: Sit down then. Relax.

MERCY: You my therapist now?

VIV: Why not, I need a new profession. You talk and I'll listen.

MERCY: Okay.

MERCY sits at the table. Lights up on JEAN, also sitting at the table.

Under the dark there is always light. (*Beat.*) Frank used to say that. He would threaten to rip my skin off and show me. (*Beat.*) He said such hateful things. Again and again. His words were like punches. (*Beat.*) I didn't know words could hurt so much.

JEAN: Sticks and stones. Sticks and stones.

MERCY turns to VIV.

MERCY: Sometimes I'd stay at a mate's house. Most times I would be at home. Him and mum would be in the bedroom. I could hear their love-making. Twice sometimes three times a night. He used to play really loud music. All sorts. So loud my head would ache. One time, when I was alone with him, I asked him to put it down. I asked him nicely. I'm well brought up. But he puts it louder. And when I went to turn it down he…he called me names. Over and over. I don't want to fuck up, Viv.

VIV: You won't.

MERCY: I might. I might fuck up. We were doing fine. Until Frank arrived. The day he arrived, my world changed colour. He would come when he wanted and go when he wanted. He treated her like shit. But she liked shit. She was so happy that he liked her – that anyone liked her – she took more shit than a man could shovel. If my dad hadn't left, none of this would have happened.

VIV: Why did he go?

MERCY: She told him to. My dad was a lazy git, but a loveable git. Lazy but good. They had me young, before they were ripe. I was the best thing that came out of that relationship.

VIV: Then that's good. Where did she meet Frank?

MERCY: He just turned up one evening, with red roses for her and chocolates for me. And he smiled and he was nice, you know. He was charming. He said all the right things. I thought her luck had changed. I thought this man called Frank might just be the one for her. He was different. There was something between them. You could see the sparks flying off their skin. (*Beat.*) When she was looking at Frank her eyes looked like they'd been lit by a great big fuck-off star.

VIV: Did she love him?

MERCY: Must have. (*Beat.*) But to go back, and see her now. See what she's become. I don't want to, Viv.

VIV: Is that why you spat back?

Beat.

MERCY: I didn't plan it. I'm not a violent person.

Beat.

VIV: You killed someone.

Pause.

Throughout the following, JEAN applies make-up to her face while MERCY is speaking. Imperfect make-up, with no mirror.

MERCY: You know, she was the sweetest, most generous… She would get up at six, make coffee for him so it was hot when he woke up. She had a bath and put on her make-up, because he said he didn't want to look at an ugly cow in the morning or smell her night-time smell. She wore thick mascara and painted her lips so they were bright. And she walked quietly around the place, so she didn't disturb him. And I'd listen, and watch, as she walked around her home like it belonged to someone else. Like it belonged to him. Because that's how he used to act. Like he owned the place. Like fuck he did. He used to treat her like shit. Like a dog. And I had to watch. If he didn't like something she cooked for him, he'd throw it in the bin. If we were having dinner or watching TV, and he wanted to have sex, he'd click his fingers at me and I'd have to go outside and wait. And wait. So I'd go down the chip shop, get some chocolate. Keep me warm and wired. And he played music. All the time. That fucking music, made me mad. And his mouth, his mouth said words no one should say, words that no one should hear. He said a white woman needed a white man, not a man like my father. He said I was like washing that hadn't been rinsed out. I was like a stain. A big stain. I told her what he said, and she laughed.

JEAN: Frank wouldn't say something like that.

MERCY: We'll go together, mum, in the night.

JEAN: Where?

MERCY: Anywhere.

JEAN: I won't leave my yellow curtains.

MERCY: She had this china. Best plates we could have eaten off. From her mum. Proper china plates. You know. Blue and white. With a shine on them. (*Beat.*) He smashed them, one at a time. In front of her. When he'd gone she picked up all the pieces.

JEAN: One day I'll put them all back together again.

VIV: Where's your dad now?

MERCY: Somewhere hot. Playing cards and watching the stars. I'm going to find him.

VIV: Does he write to you?

MERCY: When I first got put away, he sent me cards. Love you. Once he sent flowers, but they wouldn't let me have them. Then he sent invisible thoughts, which I caught and kept in my head. They're all in here, locked away. And every day I release one. (*Pause.*) My dad used to sit to my left. And when Frank came…he sat there instead. My mother said I was like the middle of a story.

JEAN: You're the bit everyone listens to.

VIV: They're still listening.

JEAN: I've made you spicy potatoes.

MERCY: I like spicy food, but Frank liked plain. He said spicy food made me smell. So I stopped eating it. (*Beat.*) I could never understand why we stayed on, why we let him do what he did.

JEAN: I love him.

MERCY: (*To VIV.*) He loved her.

JEAN cleans the table.

But Frank was an animal. A charming animal. People thought the world of him. And just as I thought, he's all right after all, his charm would go for a walk.

Beat.

Keep this table for me, mum. I love this table.

JEAN: I know my girl.

MERCY: This table has history for me.

MERCY leans over the table, examines it, runs her finger along it, and stops when she comes to a groove.

Mum, you remember this? You remember how this got here?

JEAN: Your dad cut the bread straight onto it, and the knife sliced right through.

MERCY: You were so mad, mum.

MERCY sighs. A moment later her hand reaches the raised cigarette-burn on the table, and she stops and looks directly at her mother.

And this – this from the time you caught me smoking.

JEAN: You shouldn't have been smoking.

MERCY caresses the table.

MERCY: I love this table, mum. It's part of me. It's part of who I am.

A door opens. JEAN and MERCY turn. A door bangs.

But he comes in and he slams the door. And he sits down. He makes her take off his big boots. His feet smell of man sweat and mud, and he sees me turn my nose away and he calls me names.

VIV: What names?

MERCY: Bitch. He calls me names. Whore. And he shouts at me. Stain. And he tells me this table is his. Nigga, coon, wog, apple-girl.

JEAN: Don't say that to my girl. Don't you dare say that to my girl.

MERCY: It's all right, mum. It's all right.

JEAN: It is not all right. Nobody speaks to my girl like that. Do you hear me?

Suddenly MERCY's expression changes, she is scared.

What? What do you mean it's your table? It's not yours. You're not part of this family, you've never been part of it. You should see his hands. The size of a boxer's gloves. I'm scared of those hands.

MERCY closes her eyes.

I'm thinking happy thoughts, imagining my mum happy and beautiful, sitting at the table with my dad. My beautiful dad.

MERCY opens her eyes suddenly and quickly.

But Frank screams across at me, 'You, open your eyes and look at me when I'm talking to you.' And he tells her he loves her and when she doesn't respond he calls her names. He says he's leaving. That's it. He's going. Women like her are three-a-penny. He needs some fresh meat anyway. He looks at me and he looks at her, and he says one piece of shit is bad enough, but two. Two. And she's amazing. She doesn't cry or anything. She just waits, like she knows what's coming. Then he smiles and says, 'What's for dinner?'

JEAN: We're having steak.

MERCY: And he goes and he puts on his music. Because he knows I hate it. And he picks up his paper and he reads and he laughs at some stupid headline. And he tells me to clean the table. So I clean it, so there's not a spot on it. While she cooks I clean and he reads. And all the time the music is playing. So loud. And I'm so tired. But I'm not as tired as my mum. She's really tired. Tiredness is bad.

Pause.

VIV: Did you kill him?

Beat.

MERCY: Me? (*Pause.*) I never hurt a fly. (*Beat.*) Don't believe me?

VIV: I…

MERCY: It's the truth. I never laid a finger on him.

VIV: You must have said you did.

MERCY: I had to.

VIV: You pleaded guilty to murder?

MERCY: I had to.

VIV: You could have gone for manslaughter. Provocation.

MERCY: They might not have believed me.

VIV: You could have tried.

MERCY: I couldn't take the chance. You know the system. Plead guilty you do less time.

VIV: But you got life.

MERCY: She's my mum.

VIV: You're her child.

MERCY: I couldn't let her…not after what she'd been through. And I wanted him dead. I wanted him dead. I prayed he'd die, get run over, I don't know, something. Anything to get him out of our lives.

VIV: You did your mother's time.

MERCY: No one ever looked after my mother. No one. Not even my dad. He loved her. But her never looked after her. I'm the only one who looked after her.

VIV: You took her blame.

MERCY: Yeah. I suppose I did.

VIV: Why?

MERCY: Because I could. What are they going to do? Lock her up now? She's already locked up. I laughed at the Gov because I know something he doesn't. I'm in control. In my heart, I know the truth. I'm free.

VIV: What about your head? What about in here?

MERCY: That's the thing. In my heart I'm free, in her head, she is. She wouldn't have lasted a week inside. She'd have strung herself up, slit her wrists. But bless her, she went mad instead. She did me a favour.

Pause.

VIV: I don't know what to say.

MERCY: There's nothing to say.

VIV: Why'd you take so long to tell me?

MERCY: It's a big thing to tell someone.

VIV: That you're innocent?

MERCY: Yeah.

VIV: Isn't that what we all say?

MERCY: But some of us aren't and I really am.

VIV: You said you did it.

MERCY: I had no choice.

VIV: You always have a choice.

MERCY: Not me. (*Beat.*) You know, what I've told you, you can't tell anyone. Ever.

VIV: I won't.

MERCY: Because I don't need anyone else to know.

VIV: You could have told them the truth.

MERCY: The truth? Which truth?

VIV: If you were in France you'd probably have got off. *Crime passionelle.*

MERCY: But I'm not in France. And they don't want to hear the truth. They don't want to hear about her or me, about what he said to us or how he treated us. They can't cope with the truth. A slightly altered version always goes down well. That's what I gave them.

VIV: What's that supposed to mean?

MERCY: I wanted her to do what she did. Because if she didn't, I would have. Is that so different?

VIV: Does she know you're getting out tomorrow?

MERCY: They told her, but I don't know if she gets it.

VIV: Mercy…do you ever think what she did was wrong?

Beat.

MERCY: I'm glad Frank isn't around anymore. (*Pause.*) I'm going to have a wash. Get out of these.

VIV: I won my bet. Pear drops!

MERCY: I'll leave them by your bed. Thanks, Viv.

VIV: Go and put on your party frock.

MERCY exits, as FREHIA enters with bags of crisps and drinks, a present and card.

Did you tell Mercy about our surprise?

FREHIA: Why?

VIV: Because she knows.

FREHIA: You know, some of the girls won't eat bacon flavoured crisps. Against their religion.

VIV: Why did you get them?

FREHIA: I didn't. And most of them are past their sell by date. (*Beat.*) Like we don't read packets of crisps, like we don't know what's in them.

VIV: It's just flavouring, not the real thing.

FREHIA: Yeah, yeah, you tell that to Fatima, you tell her. (*Beat.*) I said a prayer for Mercy. She's done her time. She has been forgiven.

VIV: Oh yeah, who by?

FREHIA: The Almighty. I know. I heard him.

VIV: Him? Her? It? Whatever.

FREHIA: My God is no woman. My God is a man. And shall I tell you why? If God was a woman she'd make sure we had more than one socket in our room, so Alicia could dry her hair and Mary could straighten hers and I could plug in my fairy-lights…all at the same time.

FREHIA shows the card to VIV.

VIV: Did everyone sign it?

FREHIA: No.

VIV: Sods.

Beat.

FREHIA: You're gonna miss her, aren't you?

VIV: Yes.

FREHIA: No you won't.

VIV: What's that supposed to mean?

FREHIA: You think I don't notice things. But I do. The minute she leaves you'll forget about her.

VIV: And you won't?

FREHIA: No, I won't ever forget Mercy Fine.

MERCY enters.

VIV: Everything all right Mercy?

MERCY: Yeah.

FREHIA: Fucking great. (*Beat.*) Where are the others?

VIV: Don't know.

FREHIA: Go and find them.

VIV: You go.

FREHIA: No.

Beat. VIV urges FREHIA to go look for the others. FREHIA exits unwillingly.

MERCY: So, this is my surprise party?

VIV: It was supposed to be.

MERCY: This cake Frehia's idea?

VIV: I would have had something a little more sophisticated.

MERCY: Selfridges instead of Sainsbury's?

VIV laughs.

So who's coming?

VIV: A few of the girls.

MERCY: Governor?

VIV: He's playing squash.

MERCY: Shame.

VIV: Shame.

MERCY: I'm going to have a fuck-off pint of white wine tomorrow.

VIV: Start with a half.

MERCY: I want to get pissed.

VIV: Don't.

MERCY: Don't let Frehia have too much of that stuff. Caffeine does strange things to her head.

FREHIA enters.

FREHIA: Surprise! You excited?

MERCY: Scared.

VIV: You'll be all right.

FREHIA: All them people, and the traffic and getting used to it all. It's making my head hurt just thinking about it.

VIV: Frehia!

FREHIA: Getting back, fitting in, making friends. Meeting men.

MERCY: What to say to people.

FREHIA: Kissing men.

MERCY: How to say it. How to say, hi, I'm Mercy, without my number and history. Getting a bus. Getting my own car.

VIV: Take it slowly.

FREHIA: Like a good shag.

VIV: You'll be able to get up when you want. Watch TV when you want.

FREHIA: But you must behave.

MERCY: Where are the others?

FREHIA: You must behave.

VIV: They're coming. (*Beat.*) Frehia?

FREHIA: Yeah, yeah. I saw Mary and Alicia, they're on their way.

VIV: What about the new girl?

FREHIA shakes her head.

FREHIA: She's too upset.

VIV: The others?

FREHIA shrugs.

You know what they're like, moody lot.

FREHIA: Can we have some cake now?

VIV: Mercy?

MERCY: Not for me.

VIV: Later, Frehia.

FREHIA: Can I do my song?

VIV: Now?

MERCY: What song?

FREHIA: I wrote a song for you.

VIV: Maybe not now.

FREHIA: It's a Christmas song. Sort of.

MERCY: For me?

FREHIA: Yeah. Just for you. No music. Just me.

VIV: Mercy?

MERCY: Okay.

FREHIA: I've always been a bit…you know…good with the lyrics.

VIV: Just get it over with.

FREHIA stands, waits a moment, like she's getting it together in her head, then gives it everything she's got. And it's good.

FREHIA: Fill the decks with boughs of holly. Holly. Holly. Fill the decks with boughs of holly. Fa la la la la la la la – shoplifting, sexual abuse, physical abuse, emotional abuse. GBH, ABH, ASBOS, theft, drugs, rock n' roll. Clipping, dripping, scoring, choring, it's a crime, it's a crime. God rest ye merry gentlemen la la la la la la. Manslaughter, murder, carrying an offensive weapon, thou shalt not covet thy neighbour's wife. It's a crime. It's a crime. In America, in some states, you can't do girl on girl or boy on boy, just sweet hetero love. Some places you can't spit, can't shit on the street. Some places don't have no streets, and if you don't have no fancy pot to lay your arse on, where you supposed to drop a number two. Number three, number four. I didn't do it. I didn't do it. The holly and the ivy when they are both full grown, of all the trees that are in the yard, the holly bears the crown. Non-payment of fines, what am I supposed to do? Four small kids and all you say is stop getting pregnant. Get a job instead. But it's easy for you. But it's…it's…easy for you. It's easy…it's easy…it's…fill the decks with boughs of holly. Fa la la la la la la la – (*Beat.*) la. (*Beat.*) Can I have some cake now?

MERCY: Yeah.

FREHIA takes a piece of Spongebob, realises she would rather have a packet of crisps.

The conversation is becoming strained. The women don't know what to say, so small-talk ensues.

What you two doing tomorrow?

VIV: I'll be in the library.

FREHIA: Charity shop.

MERCY: Right.

FREHIA: And you?

MERCY: Dunno. Looking at a different piece of sky.

FREHIA: It's all the same you know.

VIV: She means metaphorically.

MERCY: *Mais oui.*

FREHIA: Don't forget us.

MERCY: I won't.

FREHIA: Send us a postcard. Wish you were here and all that. Only you won't wish we were there, will you, you won't. No one ever does.

VIV: How are you getting to the station?

MERCY: Walking.

VIV: We'll get someone to take you.

FREHIA: It's gonna be strange. All those cars. They do my head in. All those people. All coming at you. Straight at you.

VIV: Shut up!

MERCY: Did you take your pills?

FREHIA: Yeah. I ain't stupid. Just bi-polar. Open it now.

MERCY: What?

FREHIA: We got you a little something. Me and Viv. Well, Viv really, cos I ain't got no money. But she's loaded.

MERCY: Now?

FREHIA: Yeah.

VIV: She doesn't have to.

MERCY: I can do it now.

MERCY rips open the present. It's a bottle of Chanel N⁰5.

Thanks. (*Beat.*) Thanks.

MERCY opens the card. There are four signatures on it and one from Governor Smith. MERCY reads.

VIV: We couldn't get everyone to sign it.

FREHIA: But they will. Before you go.

MERCY: It's all right.

FREHIA: See what the Gov says.

MERCY reads and giggles.

MERCY: 'Well done Mercy Fine. (*Beat.*) I never want to see you again.' (*Beat.*) Feeling's mutual. (*Pause.*) This'll be you soon, Viv. In your front room with a cup of Earl Grey and a posh biscuit.

FREHIA: A Hob Snob.

MERCY: Look, do you mind if I go for a bit of a walk.

VIV: The others will be here soon.

FREHIA: I could do my song again.

MERCY: Sorry, I…I think I just want to…you know…get my head around it all.

VIV: We'll give you a good send-off in the morning.

MERCY: I want to go alone. The way I came in. Thanks, for this.

FREHIA: We wouldn't want you to smell bad.

MERCY: I'll leave the pear drops by your bed.

All three just stand.

FREHIA: Good luck.

VIV: Look after yourself.

MERCY: You too.

VIV: Write and let me know how you are.

They just hold it for a moment. These women are not used to hugging each other, so they don't. MERCY exits with her present and card. FREHIA and VIV look at each other.

FREHIA: What do we do with this lot?

VIV: Share it out.

FREHIA: No way.

FREHIA gathers everything up in the tablecloth, carries the cake-box separately and exits with the lot. VIV looks around the room. Blackout.

19

From the darkness, there is a gradual rise of brilliant sunshine. As the lights come up, MERCY is standing in the Drawing Room with her case. She is made up, her lips are a brilliant colour. She looks straight ahead of her. An officer's voice bursts out over the tannoy.

OFFICER: (*Off.*) Will Mercy Fine please go to the main gate. Mercy Fine. To the main gate please.

Beat.

MERCY looks around the room. She takes a decoration from the tree and puts it in her pocket.

Over the tannoy the voice is louder and more urgent.

(*Off.*) Will Mercy Fine go to the main gate now. Mercy Fine. To the main gate.

MERCY: *Au revoir.*

MERCY stands in the doorway as the lights fade.

20

Lights up. JEAN, is her chair. MERCY stands in the doorway. Lights down as music plays.

The End.

WWW.OBERONBOOKS.COM

9 781840 026375